Rita Mulcahy's
Hot Topics

Flashcards for Passing the
Project Managment (PMP)® and
Certified Associate in Project Management (CAPM)® Exams

Eighth Edition

Aligned with *A Guide to the
Project Management Body of
Knowledge (PMBOK® Guide)*
— *Fifth Edition*

Printed in the United States of America
Ninth Printing

ISBN 978-1-932735-67-3

PMI, PMP, PMBOK, CAPM, and OPM3 are registered marks of the Project Management Institute, Inc.

This publication contains material from *A Guide to the Project Management Body of Knowledge (PMBOK® Guide)—Fifth Edition*, which is copyrighted material of, and owned by, Project Management Institute, Inc. (PMI), copyright 2013. This publication has been developed and reproduced with the permission of PMI. Unauthorized reproduction of this material is strictly prohibited.

This publication uses the following terms copyrighted by the Project Management Institute, Inc.: Project Management Institute (PMI)®, Project Management Professional (PMP)®, *A Guide to the Project Management Body of Knowledge (PMBOK® Guide)*, Certified Associate in Project Management (CAPM)®, and Organizational Project Management Maturity Model (OPM3)®.

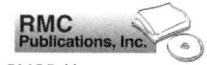

RMC Publications, Inc.
Phone: 952.846.4484
Fax: 952.846.4844
Email: info@rmcls.com
Web: www.rmcls.com

WARNING: This is not a stand-alone product! You will need other review materials in order to pass the PMP or CAPM exam. We make no warranties or representations that use of these materials will result in passage of either exam. This book is designed to work with the book *PMP® Exam Prep, Eighth Edition*, and the book *CAPM® Exam Prep, Third Edition*. Both books are available at www.rmcproject.com. Use the chapter references on each *Hot Topics* flashcard to find further information in the *PMP® Exam Prep* or *CAPM® Exam Prep* books.

TABLE OF CONTENTS

This book has been updated for the
PMBOK® Guide, Fifth Edition. It is a
portable reference to the Hot Topics
on the PMP and CAPM exams, to be
used to improve test-taking speed and
information recall.

Read the front of each page and see if
you can recall the items on the back of
the page and know what they mean. If
studying for the PMP exam, review Hot
Topics you are unfamiliar with in the
book *PMP® Exam Prep, Eighth Edition,*
and the *PMBOK® Guide, Fifth Edition.*
If you are studying for the CAPM exam,
review Hot Topics you are unfamiliar
with in the book *CAPM® Exam Prep,
Third Edition,* and the *PMBOK® Guide,
Fifth Edition.* An audio version of Hot
Topics is also available on CD.

ABOUT RMC

Founded in 1991 by Rita Mulcahy, RMC Project Management is the innovator in project management training and professional development. Over the last two decades, hundreds of thousands of project managers in over 50 regions of the world have utilized one of our professional development resources, classes, or e-Learning courses to prepare for certification, expand their project management knowledge, and further their careers. Today, we offer a wide range of innovative classes and products for beginning and advanced project managers—as well as those seeking a project management certification.

When people ask what makes RMC different than other companies, our answer is threefold: 1) we minimize the number of hours needed to learn, 2) we maximize knowledge delivery and retention in everything we do, and 3) we communicate knowledge that is immediately applicable by project managers in the real world. A simple, yet powerful philosophy.

See us at www.rmcproject.com

PMP EXAM PREP PRODUCTS

Rita Mulcahy's™ *PMP® EXAM PREP, EIGHTH EDITION*
This is the best-selling guide to the PMP exam, and is currently used in more than 50 regions of the world. This Course in a Book® contains review material, exercises, activities, games, and insider tips, and decreases study time.

Rita Mulcahy's™ *PM FASTRACK® EXAM SIMULATION SOFTWARE*
PM FASTrack® offers more than 1,500 questions in several testing modes.

What is the definition of a project?

Temporary

Creates a unique product, service, or result

What is operational work?

Ongoing work to support the business
and systems of the organization

What is the definition of a program?

What is the definition of a portfolio?

Program: A group of interrelated projects, managed in a coordinated way

Portfolio: A group of programs, individual projects, and related operational work to achieve a specific strategic business goal

What is organizational project
management (OPM)?

What are its benefits?

A framework for keeping the organization focused on its overall strategy

Provides direction for how portfolios, programs, projects, and other organizational work should be prioritized, managed, executed, and measured to best achieve the firm's strategic goals

What is OPM3®?

A PMI model designed to help organizations determine their level of maturity in project management

What is a project management office (PMO)?

What are three possible formats for a PMO?

A department that centralizes and
standardizes the management of projects

Supportive

Controlling

Directive

What are project constraints?

Time

Cost

Risk

Scope

Quality

Resources

Customer satisfaction

Constraints are used to help evaluate
competing demands

Who are project stakeholders?

Anyone whose interests may be positively or negatively impacted by the project, including:

- Project manager
- Customer
- Sponsor
- Performing organization
- Other departments or groups within the organization
- Team members
- Team members' functional or operational managers
- Sellers
- Funding sources
- End users
- PMO

What are three primary forms of
organizational structure?

Project Management Framework

Functional

Projectized

Matrix

What is a functional organization?

The organization is grouped by areas of specialization (e.g., accounting, marketing)

What is a projectized organization?

The organization is grouped by project

The team has no department to go to at project end

The project manager has total control of the resources

What is a matrix organization?

A blend of functional and projectized organization where the team members have two bosses (the project manager and functional manager)

What is a strong matrix organization?

A matrix organization where the balance of power rests with the project manager instead of the functional manager

What is a weak matrix organization?

What role might the project manager play in a weak matrix?

A matrix organization where the balance of power rests with the functional manager instead of the project manager

A project expediter or project coordinator

What is a balanced matrix organization?

A matrix organization where power is equally balanced between the project manager and the functional manager

What is a project-based organization?

A temporary framework for projects created to circumvent any obstacles inherent in the organization's existing structure (whether functional, projectized, or matrix)

What are enterprise environmental factors?

When are they used?

The organization's culture and existing systems that the project will have to deal with or can make use of

They are used throughout the project management process

What are organizational process assets?

When are they used?

Company processes and procedures

Historical information

Lessons learned

They are used throughout the project management process

What is historical information?

Records of past projects, including lessons learned, used to plan and manage future projects

Records of the current project that will become part of organizational process assets

What is a project management
information system?

The automated system to submit and track changes and monitor and control project activities

What do lessons learned describe?

How are lessons learned used?

What went right, what went wrong, and what would be done differently if the project could be redone

Used in planning the project

Used by other projects in the future

What is work performance data?

Measurements and details about
activities gathered during project work
(executing)

What is work performance information?

Work performance data analyzed to make sure it conforms to the project management plan and to assess what it means for the project as a whole

What are work performance reports?

Work performance information
organized into reports that are
distributed to the stakeholders

What is a product life cycle?

The cycle of a product's life from conception to withdrawal from the marketplace

What is a project life cycle?

What you need to do to COMPLETE the work (produce the deliverables of the project)

It varies by type of product, industry, and the organization's preferences

Describe a plan-driven project.

Has a predictive life cycle in which scope, schedule, and cost are determined in detail early in the life of the project, before the work begins to produce the project deliverables

Describe a change-driven project.

Uses iterative, incremental, or adaptive (agile) life cycles

Has varying levels of early planning for scope, schedule, and cost

What is the project management process?

What efforts are included in this process?

What you need to do to MANAGE the work

Includes the management efforts of:
- Initiating
- Planning
- Executing
- Monitoring and controlling
- Closing

What occurs during the initiating
process group?

Formal authorization of a project or phase

Project manager is provided with the authority and information necessary to begin the project

Stakeholders are identified and analyzed

The project vision is created

What occurs during the planning
process group?

Determine whether the project objectives, as stated in the project charter, can be achieved

Determine how the project will be accomplished

What occurs during the executing
process group?

Work defined in the project management plan is completed to meet project objectives

What occurs during the monitoring and controlling process group?

Project performance is measured against the project management plan

Variances are determined and addressed

Change requests are approved, including corrective and preventive actions and defect repair

What occurs during the closing process group?

Acceptance of the final product of the project is obtained and documented

Lessons learned are completed

Files are indexed and archived

Which process group must be completed
in a certain order?

Planning is the only process group with a set order

What does "input" mean?

Project Management Processes

"What do I need before I can...."

What does "output" mean?

"What will I have when I am done with...."

What is the process of integration
management?

Integration Management

Develop Project Charter

Develop Project Management Plan

Direct and Manage Project Work

Monitor and Control Project Work

Perform Integrated Change Control

Close Project or Phase

What is the Develop Project Charter process?

What is its key output?

Creating the project charter, which formally establishes the project and gives the project manager authority to spend money and commit resources to the project

Output: Project charter

What is the Develop Project
Management Plan process?

What is its output?

The process of creating a project management plan that is bought into, approved, realistic, and formal

Output: Project management plan

What are the key outputs of the Direct and Manage Project Work process?

Deliverables

Work performance data

Change requests

Updates to the project management plan and project documents

What are the key outputs of the Monitor and Control Project Work process?

Change requests

Work performance reports

Updates to the project management plan
and project documents

What are the key outputs of the Perform
Integrated Change Control process?

Approved change requests

Change log

Updates to the project management plan
and project documents

What are the key outputs of the Close
Project or Phase process?

Final product or service

Formal acceptance of project or phase

Lessons learned and other organizational
process assets updates

Explain the project manager's role as an integrator.

Integration Management

Making sure all the pieces of the project are properly coordinated and put together into one cohesive whole

What are the two major categories of project selection methods?

Benefit measurement (comparative)

Constrained optimization
(mathematical)

What are the economic models for
selecting a project?

Present value

Net present value

Internal rate of return

Payback period

Cost-benefit analysis

Define present value.

The value in today's dollars of a future cash flow

Define net present value (NPV).

How is it interpreted?

The present value of total benefits (income or revenue) minus costs over a series of time periods

Generally, if the NPV of a project is positive, the investment is a good choice unless an even better investment opportunity exists

Define internal rate of return (IRR).

How is it interpreted?

The rate at which a project's inflows and outflows are equal (i.e., the rate an investment in the project will return)

The higher the IRR, the better

Define payback period.

How is it interpreted?

The length of time required for the organization to recover its investment in the project (before the project starts yielding profit)

The shorter the payback period, the better

Define cost-benefit analysis.

What is the result of this analysis?

How is it interpreted?

Comparing the expected costs of a project to its potential benefits (revenue)

The benefit cost ratio (BCR)

The higher the BCR, the better

Define opportunity cost.

The opportunity given up by selecting one project over another (i.e., the value of the project not selected)

What are sunk costs?

Expended costs

Sunk costs should not be considered when deciding whether to continue a troubled project

Define the law of diminishing returns.

After a certain point, adding more input will not result in a proportional increase in productivity

Define working capital.

Current assets minus current liabilities

The amount of money the company has available to invest, including investment in projects

What are the two types of depreciation?

Straight line depreciation: Depreciate the same amount each time period

Accelerated depreciation: Depreciate an amount greater than straight line each time period

What is the project statement of work?

Describes need, product scope, and how the project fits into the organization's or the customer's strategic plan

Created by the customer/sponsor before the project starts

Later refined in the project scope statement

What is a project charter?

A document issued by the sponsor during project initiating that:

- Formally recognizes (authorizes) the existence of the project
- Gives the project manager authority to spend money and commit resources to the project
- Provides the objectives, high-level requirements, and success criteria for the project
- Identifies the constraints and high-level risks for the project
- Uncovers assumptions about the project
- Links the project to the ongoing work of the organization

What is a business case?

The project purpose and justification

Explains why the project was selected, how it fits into the organization's strategic goals, and how it will bring business value to the organization

What is included in a project
management plan?

Project management processes for the project

Management plans for knowledge areas

Scope, schedule, and cost baselines

Requirements management plan

Change management plan

Configuration management plan

Process improvement plan

What are project documents?

Any documents used to manage a project that aren't part of the project management plan, including:

- Project charter
- Project statement of work
- Procurement statement of work
- Agreements and contracts
- Stakeholder register
- Requirements documentation
- Activity list
- Quality metrics
- Risk register
- Issue log
- Change log
- Any other such documentation

What are baselines?

The parts of the project management plan against which actual project performance is measured

What three elements make up the
performance measurement baseline?

Schedule baseline

Scope baseline

Cost baseline

What is a configuration management plan?

A plan to make sure everyone knows what version of the scope, schedule, and other components of the project management plan are the latest versions

It defines how you will manage changes to the deliverables and processes and the resulting documentation

What is a change management plan?

A system of formal procedures, set up in advance, defining how project deliverables and documentation are controlled, changed, and approved

What is a change control board?

Who might be on a change control board?

The group responsible for reviewing and approving or rejecting change requests

May include project manager, customer, experts, sponsor, functional managers, and others

For the exam, assume that all projects have change control boards

What are change requests?

When are they approved?

Formal requests to change parts of the project after the project management plan is approved

Perform Integrated Change Control

What are corrective actions?

Actions taken to bring expected future project performance in line with the project management plan

What are preventive actions?

Actions taken to deal with anticipated or possible deviations from the performance measurement baseline and other metrics

What is defect repair?

Rework required when a component of the project does not meet specifications

What is a kickoff meeting?

When does it occur?

A meeting of all parties to the project (all project stakeholders, including sellers) to make sure everyone is "on the same page"

At the end of the planning process group

What is a work authorization system?

The project manager's system for authorizing the start of work packages or activities

It ensures work is done at the right time and in the proper sequence

What is the definition of product scope?

The requirements related to the product of the project

What is the definition of project scope?

The work the project will do to deliver
the product of the project

What is the process of scope
management?

Plan Scope Management

Collect Requirements

Define Scope

Create WBS

Validate Scope

Control Scope

What is the definition of scope management?

Scope Management

Defining what work is required and then making sure all of that work, and only that work, is included in the project

What are the key outputs of the Plan
Scope Management process?

Scope management plan

Requirements management plan

What are the key outputs of the Collect
Requirements process?

Requirements documentation

Requirements traceability matrix

What is the key output of the Define Scope process?

Scope Management

Project scope statement

What are the key outputs of the Create
WBS process?

Work breakdown structure (WBS)

WBS dictionary

Scope baseline (the WBS and WBS dictionary are components of the scope baseline)

What are the key outputs of the Validate
Scope process?

Work performance information

Accepted deliverables

Change requests

Updates to project documents

What are the key outputs of the Control
Scope process?

Work performance information

Change requests

Updates to the project management plan
and project documents

Name several requirements-gathering techniques.

Reviewing historical records
Interviewing
Focus groups
Facilitated workshops
Brainstorming
Nominal group technique
Multi-criteria decision analysis
Mind maps
Affinity diagrams
Questionnaires and surveys
Observation
Prototypes
Benchmarking
Context diagrams
Group decision making

What is the value of a requirements traceability matrix?

What requirement attributes might be recorded in this document?

Helps link requirements to objectives and/or other requirements to make sure the project meets strategic goals

Requirement identification number

Source of the requirement

Who is assigned to manage the requirement

Status of the requirement

What is a project scope statement?

What are the key items included in a project scope statement?

A description of the project deliverables and the work required to create those deliverables

Product scope

Project scope

Deliverables (for the product and the project)

Acceptance criteria

What is not part of the project

Assumptions and constraints

Product analysis is part of which scope management process?

Scope Management

Define Scope

When is a work breakdown structure
(WBS) created, and what is it used for?

Created during project planning by the team and used to define or decompose the project into smaller, more manageable pieces

Used to help determine project staffing, estimating, scheduling, and risk management

What is decomposition?

Subdividing the major deliverables into smaller, more manageable components

What is a WBS dictionary?

A description of the work to be done for each work package

How are work packages different from activities?

Activities are generated from each work package

Work packages are shown in a WBS

Activities are shown in an activity list and network diagram

What is the Validate Scope process?

When is it done?

The process of gaining formal acceptance of the deliverables by the customer or sponsor

During project monitoring and controlling and at the end of each phase of the project life cycle

What makes up the scope baseline?

Scope Management

Project scope statement

WBS

WBS dictionary

What is the process of time management?

Plan Schedule Management

Define Activities

Sequence Activities

Estimate Activity Resources

Estimate Activity Durations

Develop Schedule

Control Schedule

What is the key output of the Plan
Schedule Management process?

Schedule management plan

What are the key outputs of the Define
Activities process?

Time Management

Activity list

Activity attributes

Milestone list

What are the key outputs of the
Sequence Activities process?

Network diagrams

Updates to project documents

What are some of the key outputs of the Estimate Activity Resources process?

Activity resource requirements

Resource breakdown structure

What are the key outputs of the Estimate Activity Durations process?

Activity duration estimates

Updates to project documents

What does the Develop Schedule process involve?

What are some of its key outputs?

Creating a project schedule that is bought into, approved, realistic, and formal

Project schedule

Schedule baseline

Updates to the project management plan and project documents

What are the key outputs of the Control Schedule process?

Work performance information

Schedule forecasts

Change requests

What are the four types of logical relationships between activities in the precedence diagramming method?

Finish-to-start (FS): An activity must finish before the successor can start

Start-to-start (SS): An activity must start before the successor can start

Finish-to-finish (FF): An activity must finish before the successor can finish

Start-to-finish (SF): An activity must start before the successor can finish

What are mandatory dependencies?

What are discretionary dependencies?

Mandatory: The order in which activities MUST be done, due to the inherent nature of the work; also called "hard logic"

Discretionary: The order in which the organization has CHOSEN that activities be performed; also called "preferred," "preferential," or "soft logic"

What are external dependencies?

What are internal dependencies?

External: Dependencies based on the needs of a party OUTSIDE the project

Internal: Dependencies based on the needs of the project; may be under the control of the project team

What is a lag?

What is a lead?

Lag: Waiting time inserted between activities

Lead: How soon an activity can start before its predecessor activity is completed

What is a resource breakdown structure?

An organizational chart or table showing identified resources, organized by category and type

How does a schedule model differ from
a schedule?

The schedule model consists of all the project data that will be used to calculate the schedule, such as the activities, dependencies, leads and lags, etc.

The project schedule is the output of the schedule model—this refers to the final, printed dates that make up the schedule that becomes the baseline and part of the project management plan

What is the critical path?

What is the near-critical path?

Critical: The longest path through the network diagram

Near-critical: The path closest in length to the critical path

How does the critical path help us manage the project?

It shows the project manager the shortest time in which the project can be completed

It shows the project manager where to focus his or her time

It is used in compressing or adjusting the schedule

Define total float, free float, and project float.

Total float: The amount of time an activity can be delayed without delaying the project end date or an intermediary milestone

Free float: The amount of time an activity can be delayed without delaying the early start date of its successor(s)

Project float: The amount of time the project can be delayed without affecting the project's required end date

What are the two formulas for
calculating float?

Late start – Early start

OR

Late finish – Early finish

What are the methods that can be used
to compress a schedule?

Crashing

Fast tracking

What is crashing?

Adding or adjusting resources in order to compress the schedule while maintaining the original project scope

What is fast tracking?

Compressing the schedule by doing
more critical path activities in parallel

What is the critical chain method?

A schedule network analysis tool that
builds in buffers at critical milestones

What is reestimating?

Estimating the project again after planning to make sure you can still meet the end date, budget, or other objectives, and adjusting the project if you cannot

What is resource optimization?

Finding ways to adjust the use of resources

What is resource leveling?

A resource optimization technique that keeps the amount of resources used for each time period constant, resulting in a more stable level of resources and a longer project duration

What is resource smoothing?

A modified form of resource leveling, where resources are leveled only within the limits of the float of their activities, so the completion dates of activities are not delayed

What is the schedule baseline?

The approved version of the schedule model, along with any approved changes, used to measure project schedule performance

What are the main presentation formats
for a schedule?

Network diagrams

Bar charts

Milestone charts

What do network diagrams show?

Dependencies (logical relationships) between activities

How project activities will flow from beginning to end

Network diagrams may also be used to determine the critical path

What do simple bar charts show?

Project schedule or project status

What do milestone charts show?

High-level project status

What is Monte Carlo analysis?

A schedule network analysis technique used to simulate the project to determine the likelihood that the project will be completed by a specific date or for a specific cost

Also used in Perform Quantitative Risk Analysis to determine the overall level of risk on the project

What is the process of cost management?

Plan Cost Management

Estimate Costs

Determine Budget

Control Costs

What is the key output of the Plan Cost Management process?

Cost Management

Cost management plan

What are the key inputs to the Estimate
Costs process?

Cost management plan

Scope baseline

Project schedule

Human resource management plan

Risk register

Enterprise environmental factors

Organizational process assets

What are the key outputs of the Estimate Costs process?

Cost Management

Activity cost estimates

Basis of estimates

Updates to project documents

What are the key outputs of the
Determine Budget process?

Cost baseline

Project funding requirements

Updates to project documents

What are the key outputs of the Control Costs process?

Work performance information

Cost forecasts

Change requests

Updates to project management plan
and project documents

What are the main approaches to cost or schedule estimating?

One-point estimating

Analogous estimating

Bottom-up estimating

Parametric estimating

Three-point estimating

What is analogous estimating?

Top-down estimating that uses expert judgment and historical information to predict the future (for example, "The last three projects cost $25,000, or took six months, and so should this one")

What is bottom-up estimating?

Creating estimates based on the details of the project (e.g., from the bottom of the work breakdown structure), which are then rolled up into project estimates

What is parametric estimating?

Calculating estimates by looking at the relationships between variables on an activity (e.g., cost per line of code, hours per installation), based on historical information, industry requirements, standard metrics, or other sources

What is earned value measurement, and how is it used?

A method of measuring project performance that looks at the value earned for work accomplished, by reviewing project performance against the scope, schedule, and cost baselines

It can be used to predict future cost performance and project completion dates

What is the typical range for a rough
order of magnitude (ROM) estimate?

Cost Management

−25 to +75 percent from actual

What is the typical range for a budget estimate?

Cost Management

−10 percent to +25 percent from actual

What is the typical range for a definitive estimate?

+/–10 percent from actual

What is the difference between a cost budget and a cost baseline?

The cost budget adds management
reserves to the cost baseline

What is the formula for cost variance?

Cost Management

$$EV - AC = CV$$

What is the formula for schedule
variance?

Cost Management

$$EV - PV = SV$$

What is the formula for cost
performance index?

$$CPI = \frac{EV}{AC}$$

Cost Management

What is the formula for schedule performance index?

$$SPI = \frac{EV}{PV}$$

Cost Management

What are the formulas for estimate at
completion?

$$AC + \text{Bottom-up ETC} = EAC$$

$$\frac{BAC}{CPI^C} = EAC$$

$$AC + (BAC - EV) = EAC$$

$$AC + \frac{(BAC - EV)}{(CPI^C \times SPI^C)} = EAC$$

What is the formula for estimate to complete?

$$EAC - AC = ETC$$

Cost Management

What is the formula for variance at completion?

Cost Management

$$BAC - EAC = VAC$$

What is the formula for to-complete performance index?

$$\frac{(BAC - EV)}{(BAC - AC)} = TCPI$$

How do variable costs differ from fixed costs?

Variable costs vary with the amount of production or work done on the project

Fixed costs do not vary with the amount of production or work done on the project

What is a direct cost?

What is an indirect cost?

Direct cost: A cost that is directly attributable to the project

Indirect cost: Overhead costs or costs incurred for more than one project

What does life cycle costing mean?

Cost Management

Considering costs over the entire life of the product, not just the cost of the project to create the product

What is value analysis?

Finding a less costly way of doing essentially the same work (also known as value engineering)

What is the process of quality management?

Plan Quality Management

Perform Quality Assurance

Control Quality

What are the key outputs of the Plan
Quality Management process?

Quality Management

Quality management plan

Quality metrics

Quality checklists

Process improvement plan

Updates to project documents

What are the key outputs of the Perform Quality Assurance process?

Change requests

Updates to standards, processes, and quality systems (organizational process assets)

Updates to project management plan and project documents

What are the key outputs of the Control Quality process?

Quality control measurements

Validated changes

Work performance information

Updates to project management plan
and project documents

Change requests

Lessons learned (part of updates to
organizational process assets)

Verified deliverables

What is the definition of quality?

The degree to which the project fulfills requirements

How does quality differ from grade?

Whereas quality is the degree to which requirements are fulfilled, grade refers to a general category or classification for a deliverable or resource that indicates common function, but varying technical specifications

What does gold plating mean?

Adding extra items and services to customer deliverables that do not necessarily contribute added value or quality

What is marginal analysis?

An analysis to determine when optimal quality is reached—to determine the point where incremental benefits or revenue from improving quality equals the incremental cost to secure it

What is a process improvement plan?

A plan for analyzing the processes used on the project to improve them, looking for ways to decrease defects, save time and money, and increase customer satisfaction

What are quality metrics?

Specific measures of quality to be used on the project in the Perform Quality Assurance and Control Quality processes

What does continuous improvement
mean?

The ongoing enhancement of a product or service through small, continuous improvements in quality

How much inventory is maintained in a just in time (JIT) environment?

How does this affect attention to quality?

Little inventory is maintained

It forces attention to quality

What does ISO 9000 stand for?

International Organization for Standardization (ISO) quality standards that help organizations ensure that they have quality procedures and are following them

What is the definition of total quality management, or TQM?

A comprehensive management philosophy that encourages companies to find ways to continuously improve the quality of business practices, products, and services at every level of the organization

Why is "prevention over inspection" important?

Because the cost of avoiding or
preventing mistakes is much less than
the cost of correcting them

What does mutual exclusivity mean?

Two events are said to be mutually
exclusive if they cannot both occur in
a single trial (for example, you can't get
both a 5 and a 6 on a single roll of a die)

What is statistical independence?

The probability of event "B" occurring does not depend on event "A" occurring (for example, the outcome of a second roll of a die is not dependent on the outcome of the first roll)

What is a normal distribution curve?

A symmetric bell-shaped frequency distribution curve used to measure variation

This is the most common probability distribution

What does sigma signify in a process?

What's another name for sigma?

How much variance from the mean
has been established as permissible in a
process

Standard deviation

What do 3 sigma and 6 sigma refer to?

These are commonly used as quality standards

- 3 sigma: +/– 3 standard deviations from the mean
- 6 sigma: +/– 6 standard deviations from the mean

6 sigma is a higher quality standard than 3 sigma

What is the difference between a
population and a sample?

Population: The total number of individual members, items, or elements comprising a uniquely defined group (e.g., all women)

Sample: A statistically valid subset of population members (e.g., women randomly chosen to represent the population)

Who has responsibility for quality on a project?

Although team members must inspect
their own work, the project manager has
the ultimate responsibility for quality

What are the impacts of poor quality?

Increased costs

Decreased profits

Low morale

Low customer satisfaction

Increased risk

Rework

Schedule delays

What are examples of costs
of conformance and costs of
nonconformance?

Costs of conformance:
- Quality training
- Studies
- Surveys
- Efforts to ensure everyone knows the processes to use to complete their work

Costs of nonconformance:
- Rework
- Scrap
- Inventory costs
- Warranty costs
- Lost business

What are costs of nonconformance associated with?

Which should be greater, the costs of conformance or nonconformance?

Costs of nonconformance are associated with poor quality

The costs of conformance should be less than the costs of nonconformance

What are the seven basic quality tools
(7QC)?

Cause and effect diagram

Flowchart

Checksheet

Pareto diagram

Histogram

Control chart

Scatter diagram

What is a quality checklist?

A list of items to inspect, a list of steps to perform, or a picture of an item to be inspected, with space to note any defects found

How does a checksheet differ from a quality checklist?

Although a checksheet is a type of checklist, its primary purpose is to gather data

The quality checklist is intended to help verify a required action has taken place or item has been included

What is a cause and effect diagram?

A graphical tool that helps determine the possible root causes of a problem

It is also called a fishbone or Ishikawa diagram

What does a flowchart show?

How a process or system flows from beginning to end, how the elements interrelate, alternative paths the process can take, and how the process translates inputs into outputs

What is a Pareto chart?

A histogram that arranges the results from most frequent to least frequent to help identify which root causes are resulting in the most problems

What does a scatter diagram show?

The relationship between two variables

What is a control chart?

A specialized trend chart that documents whether a measured process is in or out of statistical control

What are control limits?

The acceptable range of variation on a
control chart

What are the specification limits on a control chart?

The customer's definition of acceptable product/service characteristics and tolerances

How do we define a process as statistically out of control?

What does out of control mean?

A data point falls outside the upper or lower control limit, or there are nonrandom data points

There is a lack of consistency and predictability in the process

What is the rule of seven?

What does it signify?

Seven consecutive data points appearing on a control chart on one side of the mean

The process is out of statistical control

What is an assignable cause/special cause variation?

A data point (or set of data points) on a control chart indicates that the measured process is out of statistical control and that the cause(s) of the event must be investigated

Define benchmarking.

Comparing your project to other projects to get ideas for improvement and to provide a benchmark for measuring quality performance

What is design of experiments?

A statistical method that allows you to experimentally change all of the important variables in a process to determine what combination will optimize overall quality

What is statistical sampling?

Inspecting by testing only part of a
population (a statistically valid sample)

Define cost-benefit analysis.

Comparing the costs of an effort to the benefits of that effort

What are some of the tools and techniques used in the Perform Quality Assurance process?

Plan Quality Management and Control
Quality tools and techniques

Process analysis

Quality audits

Affinity diagrams

Tree diagrams

Process decision program charts

Interrelationship digraphs

Matrix diagrams

Prioritization matrices

Activity network diagrams

What are quality audits?

Structured reviews of quality policies, practices, and procedures to ensure they are efficient and effective

These audits often result in lessons learned for the organization

What is the process of human resource management?

Plan Human Resource Management

Acquire Project Team

Develop Project Team

Manage Project Team

What is the key output of the Plan
Human Resource Management process?

Human resource management plan

What are the key outputs of the Acquire
Project Team process?

Project staff assignments

Resource calendars

Updates to project management plan

What is a key output of the Develop
Project Team process?

Team performance assessments
(evaluating team effectiveness)

What is a key output of the Manage
Project Team process?

Change requests

What are some key responsibilities of the sponsor on a project?

Provide information regarding the initial scope of the project

Issue the charter

Provide funding

May dictate dates

Approve the final project management plan

Approve or reject changes or authorize a change control board

Be involved in risk management

What are some key responsibilities of the team on a project?

Identify requirements, constraints, and assumptions

Create the work breakdown structure and help with project planning

Estimate activities

Participate in risk management

Complete activities

Comply with quality and communications plans

Recommend changes to the project

What are some key responsibilities of the stakeholders on a project?

Stakeholders may help:
- Identify requirements and constraints
- Plan the project
- Approve changes
- Perform the risk management process

What are some key responsibilities of functional managers on a project?

Participate in planning

Approve the final project management plan

Approve the final schedule

Assist with problems related to team member performance

Manage activities that happen within their functional area

What are the key elements of a human resource management plan?

When and how human resource requirements will be met

Roles and responsibilities

Project organization charts

Staffing management plan

What is included in a staffing management plan?

Staff acquisition plan

Resource calendars

Staff release plan

Staff training needs

Recognition and rewards

Compliance

Safety

What are some of the different types of project teams?

Dedicated

Part-time

Partnership

Virtual

What are some of the key activities
involved in developing the project team?

Hold team-building activities throughout the project

Use personnel assessment tools to learn about the team members

Obtain and provide training where needed

Establish ground rules

Give recognition and rewards

Conduct team performance assessments

What are some key activities involved in managing a project team?

Use negotiation and leadership skills

Observe what is happening

Use an issue log

Keep in touch

Conduct project performance appraisals

Be a leader

Actively look for and help resolve
conflicts that the team members cannot
resolve on their own

What is a team performance assessment?

An assessment by the project manager meant to evaluate and enhance the effectiveness of the project team

What are the different types of power?

Formal (legitimate)

Reward

Penalty (coercive)

Expert

Referent

What are some of the different types of
leadership and management styles?

Directing

Facilitating

Coaching

Supporting

Autocratic

Consultative

Consultative-
Autocratic

Consensus

Delegating

Bureaucratic

Charismatic

Democratic
(participative)

Laissez-faire

Analytical

Driver

Influencing

List the most common sources of conflict on projects, in order of most to least common.

1. Schedules

2. Project priorities

3. Resources

4. Technical opinions

5. Administrative procedures

6. Cost

7. Personality

Name some conflict resolution
techniques.

Collaborating (problem solving)

Compromising (reconciling)

Withdrawal (avoidance)

Smoothing (accommodating)

Forcing (directing)

Define collaborating (problem solving).

Define compromising (reconciling).

Collaborating: Openly discussing differences and incorporating multiple viewpoints to achieve consensus (a win-win solution)

Compromising: Finding an outcome that brings some degree of satisfaction to all parties involved (a lose-lose solution)

Define withdrawal (avoidance).

Define smoothing (accommodating).

Define forcing (directing).

Withdrawal: Postponing a decision or avoiding the problem

Smoothing: Emphasizing agreement rather than differences of opinion

Forcing: Pushing one viewpoint at the expense of another (a win-lose solution)

What are some of the project manager's
human resource responsibilities?

Determine needed resources

Negotiate for optimal available resources

Create a project team directory

Create project-related job descriptions for team members

Make sure roles and responsibilities are clear

Ensure team members obtain needed training

Create recognition and reward systems

Create a human resource management plan

What are project performance
appraisals?

Evaluations of the performance of individual team members

What is an issue log?

A record that lists the project issues, their causes and impacts on the project, the person(s) responsible for resolving each issue, the issue status, and target resolution dates

What is Maslow's theory about needs?

Maslow's hierarchy of needs states that people are motivated according to the following hierarchy of needs:

- Self-actualization
- Esteem
- Social
- Safety
- Physiological

What theories of management does
McGregor describe?

Theory X: Managers who accept this theory believe that people need to be constantly watched and micromanaged

Theory Y: Managers who accept this theory believe that people want to achieve and can direct their own efforts without supervision

What does Herzberg's theory describe?

The effects of hygiene factors and motivating agents on motivation

Hygiene factors: working conditions, salary, personal life, work relationships, security, status, etc.

Motivating agents: responsibility, self-actualization, professional growth, recognition, etc.

What is McClelland's theory of needs?

McClelland says that each person is most motivated by one of three needs:

- Achievement
- Affiliation
- Power

What are the stages of team formation
and development?

Forming

Storming

Norming

Performing

Adjourning

What is multi-criteria decision analysis?

Using a set of criteria (such as availability, cost, experience, location, skill set, knowledge, or training) to evaluate potential team members

What is the "halo effect"?

The tendency to rate people high or low on all factors because of a high or low rating on a specific factor (for example, the tendency to assume that a team member will be a great project manager because she completes all her assigned activities on time)

What is the process of communications management?

Plan Communications Management

Manage Communications

Control Communications

What is the key output of the Plan
Communications Management process?

Communications management plan

What are the key outputs of the Manage
Communications process?

Project communications

Updates to project management plan
and project documents

Updates to organizational process assets

What are the key inputs to Control
Communications?

Project management plan

Project communications

Issue log

Work performance data

Organizational process assets

What are the key outputs of the Control
Communications process?

Work performance information

Change requests

Updates to project management plan
and project documents

Updates to organizational process assets

How should communication flow on a project?

To the customer, sponsor, functional managers, team members, other stakeholders, other project managers, and to other projects

Describe the basic communication model.

Communication consists of three parts: a sender, a message, and a receiver

Each message is encoded by the sender and decoded by the receiver

Factors that affect the way the receiver decodes a message are called noise, and include environment, experience, and language

What are the components of effective communication?

What are the components of effective listening?

Effective communication:
- Nonverbal communication
- Paralingual communication
- Words

Effective listening:
- Active listening
- Giving feedback

What is paralingual communication?

Pitch and tone of voice

What are the four types of
communication?

Formal written

Formal verbal

Informal written

Informal verbal

Define interactive, push, and pull
communication methods.

Interactive: The sender provides the information and recipients receive and respond to it

Push: The sender provides the information but does not expect feedback on that information

Pull: The sender places the information in a central location and recipients are responsible for retrieving it

How much of their time do project managers spend communicating?

90 percent

What are some examples of
communication technology?

Face-to-face interactions

Telephone

Fax

Mail

Instant messaging

E-mail

What are the communication blockers that can get in the way of communicating?

Noisy surroundings

Distance

Improper encoding

Negative statements

Hostility

Language

Culture

What are some rules for effective meetings?

- Set a time limit, and keep to it
- Schedule in advance
- Meet with the team regularly, but not too often
- Have a purpose for each meeting
- Create an agenda with team input
- Distribute agenda in advance, and stick to it
- Let people know their responsibilities in advance
- Bring the right people together
- Lead the meeting with a set of rules
- Assign deliverables and time limits for assignments resulting from meetings
- Publish the meeting minutes

What is the formula for communication channels?

$$\frac{N\,(N\text{-}1)}{2}$$

Communications Management

Name some of the different types of
performance reports.

Status report

Progress report

Trend report

Forecasting report

Variance report

Earned value report

Lessons learned documentation

What is the process of risk management?

Risk Management

Plan Risk Management

Identify Risks

Perform Qualitative Risk Analysis

Perform Quantitative Risk Analysis

Plan Risk Responses

Control Risks

What is the key output of the Plan Risk Management process?

Risk management plan

What is the key output of the Identify Risks process?

Risk register

Risk Management

What key outputs of the Perform Qualitative Risk Analysis process are added to the risk register?

Risk ranking for the project

Prioritized risks and their probability and impact ratings

Risks grouped by category

List of risks requiring additional analysis and response

List of risks requiring analysis in the near term

Watch list (noncritical risks)

What key outputs of the Perform Quantitative Risk Analysis process are added to the risk register?

Prioritized list of quantified risks

Initial amount of contingency time and cost reserves needed

Possible realistic and achievable completion dates and project costs

Quantified probability of meeting project objectives

Trends in quantitative risk analysis

What key outputs of the Plan Risk Responses process are added to the risk register?

Residual risks

Contingency plans

Fallback plans

Risk owners

Secondary risks

Risk triggers

Contracts

Reserves for time and cost

What are the key outputs of the Control
Risks process?

Work performance information

Risk register updates

Change requests

Updates to the project management plan and project documents

Updates to organizational process assets

What key outputs of the Control Risks
process are added to the risk register?

Outcomes of risk reassessments and risk audits

Results of implemented risk responses

Updates to previous parts of risk management

Closing of risks that are no longer applicable

Details of what happened when risks occurred

Lessons learned

What is a risk?

A future occurrence that may or may not happen that can have a positive (opportunity) or negative (threat) impact on the project

What are the four key factors that need
to be determined for each risk?

Probability

Impact

Timing

Frequency

A person who is risk averse is:

Unwilling to take risks

Define risk appetite, risk tolerance, and risk threshold.

Risk appetite: a general, high-level description of the acceptable level of risk

Risk tolerance: a measurable amount of acceptable risk

Risk threshold: the specific point at which risk becomes unacceptable

What are the inputs to the risk management process?

Project background information and other organizational process assets

Enterprise environmental factors

Project charter, network diagram, and other project documents

Project management plan (including scope baseline and the knowledge area plans)

Time and cost estimates

Procurement documents

Stakeholder register

Risk register

Work performance data and reports

What are some examples of sources of risk?

Technical

Project management

Schedule

Cost

Quality

Scope

Resources

Customer satisfaction

What are some examples of risk
identification techniques?

Documentation reviews

Information-gathering techniques

SWOT analysis (strengths, weaknesses, opportunities, threats)

Checklist analysis

Assumptions analysis

Diagramming techniques

What are risk triggers?

Early warning signs that a risk event has occurred, or is about to occur

They let risk owners know when to take action

What is assumptions analysis?

When is it done?

Assessing the assumptions made on the project and determining whether they are valid

During Identify Risks

What is risk data quality assessment?

When is it done?

Determining how accurate, reliable, and well understood the risk information is

During Perform Qualitative Risk Analysis

What is a probability and impact matrix?

The company's standard rating system to promote a common understanding of what each risk rating means

What is sensitivity analysis?

A technique to analyze and compare the potential impacts of identified risks

What is the formula for expected
monetary value?

Probability times impact, or

$$EMV = P \times I$$

What is a decision tree?

A model of a decision to be made that includes the probabilities and impacts of future events

Who is a risk owner?

The person assigned to develop and
execute risk responses for a critical risk

What are the possible risk response strategies for threats?

Avoid: Eliminate the threat by eliminating its cause

Mitigate: Reduce the probability or impact of the threat

Transfer: Make another party responsible for the risk (outsourcing, insurance, warranties, bonds, guarantees)

Accept:
- Passive acceptance—do nothing; if it happens, it happens
- Active acceptance—develop contingency plans in advance

What are the possible risk response strategies for opportunities?

Exploit: Make sure the opportunity occurs

Enhance: Increase probability or positive impact of the risk event

Share: Allocate full or partial ownership of the opportunity to a third party

Accept: Do nothing; if it happens, it happens

What are residual risks?

Risks that remain after risk response planning

What are secondary risks?

New risks created by the implementation
of risk response strategies

How does buying insurance relate to risk response planning?

It exchanges an unknown cost impact of
a known risk for a known cost impact

It is a method to decrease project risk

How does a contract relate to risk response planning?

A contract helps allocate and mitigate risks

Risk analysis must be done before a contract is signed

What are contingency plans?

Planned responses to be implemented
when and if a risk event occurs

What are fallback plans?

Actions that will be taken if the
contingency plan is not effective

What are reserves?

What are the two kinds of reserves?

Time or cost added to the project to account for risk

Management reserve

Contingency reserve

What is a contingency reserve?

Time or cost allocated to cover known unknowns

It is included in the cost baseline

What is a management reserve?

Time or cost allocated to cover unknown unknowns

It is added to the cost baseline to get the cost budget

What are workarounds?

Unplanned responses developed to deal with the occurrence of unanticipated events or problems on a project (or to deal with risks that had been accepted because of unlikelihood of occurrence and/or minimal impact)

What are risk reassessments?

When do they occur?

Reviews of the risk management plan
and risk register

During Control Risks

What is reserve analysis?

When is it done during the risk management process?

Managing the reserves and making sure
the amount remaining is adequate

During Control Risks

What are risk audits?

Assessing the effectiveness of the risk management process and specific risk responses that have been implemented

What is the process of procurement
management?

Procurement Management

Plan Procurement Management

Conduct Procurements

Control Procurements

Close Procurements

What are the inputs to the Plan
Procurement Management process?

Project management plan

Requirements documentation

Activity resource requirements

Enterprise environmental factors

Organizational process assets

Risk register

Stakeholder register

Any procurements already in place

Project schedule

Initial cost estimates for work to be procured

What are the key outputs of the Plan Procurement Management process?

Make-or-buy decisions

Procurement management plan

Procurement statements of work

Procurement documents

Source selection criteria

Change requests

What are the key outputs of the Conduct
Procurements process?

Selected sellers

Signed contracts

Resource calendars

Change requests

Updates to project management plan and project documents

What are the key outputs of the Control Procurements process?

Substantial completion of contract requirements and deliverables

Work performance information

Change requests

Updates to project management plan and project documents

What are the key outputs of the Close
Procurements process?

Formal acceptance

Closed procurements

Updates to lessons learned and records
(part of organizational process assets)

What is an agreement?

What is a contract?

Agreement: A document or communication that outlines internal or external relationships and their intentions

Contract: A type of written or verbal agreement, typically created with an external entity, where there is some exchange of goods or services for some type of compensation (usually monetary); a contract forms the legal relationship between the entities

What is the difference between
centralized and decentralized
contracting?

Centralized: There is one procurement department, and the procurement manager handles procurements for many projects

Decentralized: A procurement manager is assigned to one project full-time and reports directly to the project manager

What are the advantages and
disadvantages of centralized contracting?

Advantages:
- Higher level of procurement expertise
- Standardized practices provide efficiency
- Clear career path in procurement management
- Continuous improvement, training, and shared lessons learned

Disadvantages:
- Procurement manager's attention is divided among many projects
- More difficult for the project manager to obtain contracting help when needed

What are the advantages and disadvantages of decentralized contracting?

Advantages:

- Project manager has easier access to contracting expertise
- Procurement manager has more loyalty to the project
- Procurement manager has a better understanding of the project needs

Disadvantages:

- No home department for the contracts person after the project
- Difficult to maintain a high level of contracting expertise
- Duplication of expertise/inefficient use of procurement resources
- Contracting processes aren't standardized
- No career path as a procurement manager in the company

What is required for a legal contract?

Offer

Acceptance

Consideration

Legal capacity

Legal purpose

What is included in a contract?

Procurement Management

Legal terms

Business terms regarding payments

Reporting requirements

Marketing literature

Proposal

Procurement statement of work

Describe the project manager's role in procurement.

Procurement Management

Understand the procurement process

Make sure the contract contains all the scope of work and project management requirements

Incorporate mitigation and allocation of risks into the contract

Help tailor the contract to the project

Be involved during contract negotiations to protect the relationship with the seller

Make sure all the work in the contract is done, not just the technical scope

Work with the procurement manager to manage changes to the contract

What is a procurement management plan?

A plan that documents how procurements will be planned, executed, controlled, and closed

What is make-or-buy analysis?

Deciding whether the performing organization should do the project work itself or outsource some or all of the work

What are the three broad categories of contracts?

Cost-reimbursable (CR)

Fixed price (FP)

Time and material (T&M)

What is a cost-reimbursable contract?

All the seller's costs are reimbursed by the buyer

What is a fixed-price contract?

There is one set fee for accomplishing all the work

What is a time and material contract?

The buyer pays on a per-hour or per-item basis

What is a cost plus fixed fee (CPFF)
contract?

All the seller's costs are reimbursed by
the buyer, and a fixed fee is negotiated
for the seller's profit

What is a cost plus percentage of cost
(CPPC) contract?

All the seller's costs are reimbursed by the buyer, and the buyer also pays a specified percentage of those costs as a fee or profit

What is a cost plus incentive fee (CPIF)
contract?

The seller's costs are reimbursed by the buyer, and the buyer and seller share any cost savings or overruns

What is a cost plus award fee (CPAF) contract?

All the seller's costs are reimbursed by the buyer, and the buyer pays a base fee plus an award amount (a bonus) based on performance

What is a fixed price incentive fee (FPIF) contract?

The buyer pays a fixed price plus an
additional fee if the seller exceeds
performance criteria stated in the
contract

What is a fixed price award fee (FPAF) contract?

The buyer pays a fixed price plus an award (paid in full or in part) based on the seller's performance level

What is a fixed price economic price adjustment (FPEPA) contract?

A fixed-price contract with a built-in economic price adjustment to cover cost increases due to future economic conditions

What is a purchase order?

A unilateral contract typically used for buying commodities

Purchase orders become contracts once they are "accepted" by the seller's fulfillment of the contract

What do incentives accomplish?

What might incentives be used for?

They align the seller's motivations with
the buyer's objectives

Time

Cost

Quality

Scope

Who has the cost risk in a cost-reimbursable contract?

Who has the cost risk in a fixed-price contract?

Cost-reimbursable: The risk is borne by the buyer

Fixed price: The risk is borne by the seller

What is the ceiling price?

The highest price the buyer will pay

It's a condition of the contract that must be agreed to by both parties before signing

What is the point of total assumption?

For fixed price incentive fee contracts,
the amount above which the seller bears
all the loss of a cost overrun

Describe the three different types of
procurement statements of work.

Performance: Conveys what the final product should accomplish

Functional: Conveys the end purpose or result (the minimum essential characteristics of the product)

Design: Conveys exactly what work is to be done and how it should be completed

What are the procurement documents?

Request for proposal (RFP)

Invitation for bid (IFB)

Request for quotation (RFQ)

A request for information (RFI) is
sometimes considered a procurement
document, though it does not really
belong in this category

What is a nondisclosure agreement?

An agreement between the buyer and
prospective sellers identifying the
information or documents they will hold
confidential and control, and who in
the organization will have access to the
confidential information

What are standard contract terms and conditions?

What are special provisions?

Standard contract terms and conditions: Terms and conditions that are used for all contracts within the company

Special provisions: Terms and conditions created for the unique needs of the project

Name common terms and conditions
that may be in a contract.

Please review the long list of terms and
conditions and what they mean in the
Procurement Management chapter of
CAPM® Exam Prep or *PMP® Exam Prep*

What is a letter of intent?

A letter from the buyer, without legal binding, saying the buyer intends to hire the seller

What does privity mean?

A contractual relationship between two or more companies

What does noncompetitive procurement mean?

The work is awarded to a single source
or a sole source without competition

What are source selection criteria?

When are these criteria created, and
when are they used?

The factors the buyer will use to evaluate (weight or score) responses from the sellers

They are created during the Plan Procurement Management process, and are used during the Conduct Procurements process to pick a seller

What is a bidder conference?

What should a project manager watch out for during a bidder conference?

A meeting with prospective sellers
to make sure they all understand the
procurement and have a chance to ask
questions

Watch for:
- Collusion
- Sellers not asking questions in front
  of the competition

Make sure all the questions and answers
are documented and distributed to all
the potential sellers

What is a qualified seller list?

A list of sellers that have been preapproved

What are the objectives of negotiation?

Obtain a fair and reasonable price

Develop a good relationship with the seller

What are some examples of negotiation tactics?

Attacks

Personal insults

Good guy/Bad guy

Deadline

Lying

Limited authority

Missing man

Fair and reasonable

Delay

Extreme demands

Withdrawal

Fait accompli

Why might there be conflict between the contract administrator and the project manager?

The contract administrator is the only one with the power to change the contract

What is a contract change control system?

A system created to control changes to the contract

What is the purpose of a procurement
performance review?

Verify that the seller is performing as they should

Identify what the buyer can do to help the seller do the work

Determine if any changes are needed to improve the buyer-seller relationship and the processes they are using

Define claims administration.

Managing claims (requests by the seller for compensation from the buyer)

What is the key function of a records
management system?

Maintain an index of contract
documentation and records so that they
can be retrieved if necessary

What occurs during the Close
Procurements process?

Product validation

Procurement negotiation

Financial closure

Procurement audit

Updates to records

Final contract performance reporting

Documentation of lessons learned

Creation of procurement file

What is a procurement audit?

A structured review of the procurement
process and identification of lessons
learned to help future procurements

What is the process of stakeholder
management?

Identify Stakeholders

Plan Stakeholder Management

Manage Stakeholder Engagement

Control Stakeholder Engagement

What is the key output of the Identify
Stakeholders process?

Stakeholder register

What is the key output of the Plan
Stakeholder Management process?

Stakeholder management plan

What are the key outputs of the Manage Stakeholder Engagement process?

Issue log

Change requests

Updates to project management plan and project documents

Lessons learned (part of updates to organizational process assets)

What are the key outputs of the Control Stakeholder Engagement process?

Change requests

Work performance information

Updates to project management plan and project documents

Lessons learned (part of updates to organizational process assets)

What should the project manager
do with stakeholders throughout the
project?

Stakeholder Management

Identify all of them

Determine their requirements

Determine their expectations

Determine their interest and influence

Plan how to manage them

Plan how to communicate with them

Manage their expectations, influence, and engagement

Communicate with them

Control communications and stakeholder engagement

What are stakeholder expectations?

Beliefs (or mental pictures of) the future

Some expectations will become requirements

Why is it important to identify all stakeholders as early as possible on a project?

Stakeholders discovered late in the project will likely request changes, which can lead to delays

What does stakeholder analysis involve?

Stakeholder Management

Identifying stakeholders, analyzing their impact and influence on the project, and identifying ways to manage those impacts

What information about stakeholders might be included in a stakeholder register?

Stakeholder Management

Name and title

Contact information

Department and supervisor

Roles and responsibilities

Major requirements and expectations

Impact and influence

Classifications

Why is it important to build good relationships with stakeholders?

Close relationships with stakeholders can provide an early warning system for problems on the project

Describe the different levels of
stakeholder engagement.

Stakeholder Management

Unaware

Resistant

Neutral

Supportive

Leading

What might be documented in a
stakeholder management plan?

Stakeholder Management

Existing and desired levels of engagement for stakeholders

Details about how stakeholders will be involved in the project

How and why specific project information will be distributed to stakeholders

Guidelines for evaluating how well the plan is meeting the needs of stakeholders and the project

How communication will be used to help manage stakeholder engagement and expectations

How does the stakeholder management plan differ from the communications management plan when it comes to documenting communication requirements?

The communications management plan emphasizes the details about the technology, methods, and models of communication—the how of communication

The stakeholder management plan explains the why of communications—why stakeholders need to receive certain information, and how the sharing of that information will help in stakeholder management

What does professional and social responsibility entail?

Note: The CAPM exam does not test this topic. For the PMP exam, be sure to carefully read the Professional and Social Responsibility chapter of PMP® Exam Prep.

Professional and Social Responsibility

Responsibility

Respect

Fairness

Honesty

What does "responsibility" in project management mean?

Professional and Social Responsibility

Make decisions based on the best interests of the company and the team

Only accept assignments you are qualified to complete

If a project is beyond your qualifications or experience, alert the sponsor before you accept the assignment

Do what you say you will do

Acknowledge your errors

Respect confidentiality and protect proprietary information

Uphold laws, including copyright laws

Report unethical behavior

What does "respect" in project
management mean?

Maintain an attitude of mutual cooperation

Respect cultural differences

Don't say things that could damage another person's reputation

Engage in good faith negotiations

Respect others

Be direct in dealing with conflict

Do not use your power or position to influence others for your own benefit

What does "fairness" in project
management mean?

Act impartially

Continuously look for and disclose conflicts of interest

Do not discriminate

Honor your duty of loyalty

Do not use your position for personal or business gain

What does "honesty" in project management mean?

Try to understand the truth

Be truthful in all communications

Create an environment where others tell the truth

Do not deceive others

Notes

Notes

Notes